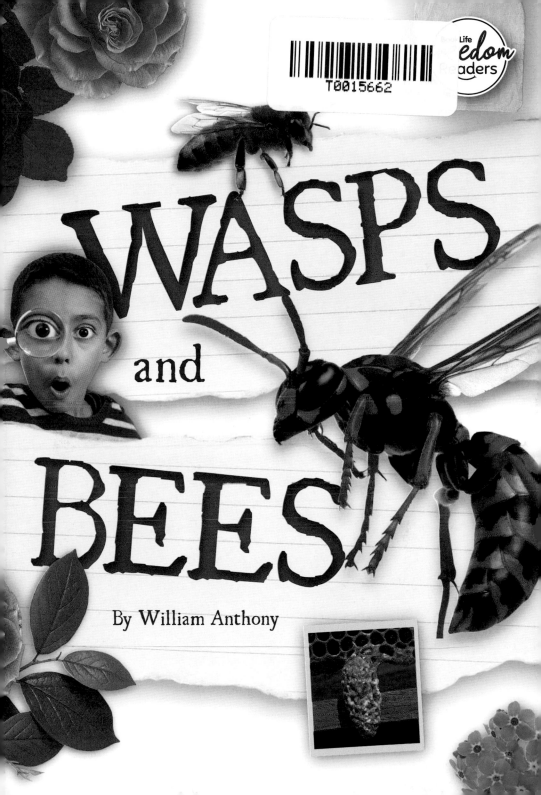

WASPS and BEES

By William Anthony

BookLife
PUBLISHING

Written by:
William Anthony

Designed by:
Amy Li

Edited by:
John Wood

QR by:
Kelby Twyman

©2022
BookLife Publishing Ltd.
King's Lynn
Norfolk, PE30 4LS

ISBN: 978-1-80155-142-7

A catalogue record for this book is available from the British Library.

All facts, statistics, web addresses and URLs in this book were verified as valid and accurate at time of writing. No responsibility for any changes to external websites or references can be accepted by either the author or publisher.

PHOTO CREDITS – Images/Videos are courtesy of Shutterstock.com. With thanks to Getty Images, Thinkstock Photo and iStockphoto.

Cover – blackzheep, Karramba Production, Ermak Oksana, ten43, Africa Studio, In Art, azure1, LanKS, irin-k, Kletr, aodaodaodaod. Recurring Images – ten43, THPStock (paper), Africa Studio (header texture), kavram (main background), In Art, Kozyreva Elena (vector bees in header), Karramba Productions (parchment), Andrey Eremin, Steve Paint (labels), azure1 (magnifying glass), Dacian G (vector phone), Ortis, LanKS, Popatov Alexander (page decoration), Ermak Oksana (doodles). P1 – blackzheep, irin-k, p2-3 – ER_09, p4-5 – Frederico Rostagno, KETPACHARA YOOSUK, p6-7 – Kovtun Petro, Nicola Dal Zotto, p8-9 – Craig Taylor, Mirko Graul, p10-11 – Krasowit, MRS.NUCH SRIBUANOY, le pur photography, p12-13 – Lehrer, p14-15 – Jack Hong, azur13, Subbotina Anna p16-17 – kosolovskyy, Lehrer, weter78, p18-19 – Jens Heidler, pixelnest, p20-21 – Computer Earth, Irina Kozorog, rtbilder, p22-23 – Gelpi, StockSmartStart, Chaikom, Mike McDonald, p24 – blackzheep.

WASPS and BEES

BookLife freedom Readers

EXPLORER TRAINING

Hi there! Do you think you could help us out? We're a team of explorers and we need a new member. However, first we need to train you up.

This book will teach you all about wasps and bees. Read through this book to earn an explorer badge at the end.

What Are WASPS and BEES?

To start off, we need to know about each part of a wasp and a bee. They're both insects. Insects have no backbones and have six legs attached to their bodies. Wasps have much thinner bodies in the middle than bees do.

Both animals have two pairs of buzzing wings to help them fly, and two antennae to help them feel the world around them. However, most wasps and bees are best known for their yellow and black patterns. Bees are usually quite hairy, while most wasps have very little hair.

Like other bugs, wasps and bees have changed over time to have lots of special body parts. Female wasps and bees both have a stinger at the tip of their body.

Both insects use their stinger to attack things that they think might hurt them or their nests. They can also alert others in their colony to attack at the same time. A colony is a group of animals living in the same place.

HOME LIFE

Wasps and bees live in different types of homes. Honey bees live in a hive, where they work as a team to raise young bees and make honey. However, most bees do not live in hives. Some bees, such as bumble bees, live in underground nests.

All types of wasp live in nests. They make their nests by chewing up wood fibres and using the sticky mixture to build a home. Look at the potter wasp below building its nest.

Meet the
COLONY

Many bees live on their own, but some bees live in colonies. Honey bees are colony bees, and they all work together. In each colony there are workers, drones and a queen.

Each colony has one queen, who gives birth to other bees. Drones are males and they mate with the queen. Worker bees are female, and they gather food and look after young bees.

HIVE MIND

Honey bees work together to keep their hive running well. Each bee knows its job in the team. One of the most important jobs is collecting nectar and pollen. Nectar and pollen are found in plants.

Worker bees leave their hive to collect nectar and pollen from different plants. Nectar is a sugary liquid and pollen is like powder. Honey bees collect them both for a very important reason – food.

Finding a
FEAST

Pollen is mixed with nectar to make bee bread. This is used to feed many of the young bees while they grow up. Adult bees eat honey.

Bee bread

Honey is made from nectar. Nectar has water in it, so the bees pass it to each other using their mouths until most of the water has gone. It turns into honey, and it is stored in the hive.

This wasp is eating a strawberry.

Wasps do not eat the same food as bees. They are omnivores, which means they eat both plants and other animals. Most wasps will eat a mixture of plants, nectar and other insects.

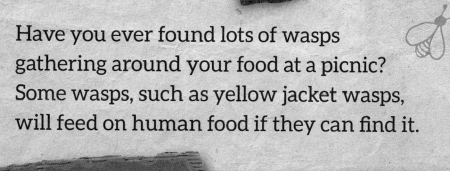

Have you ever found lots of wasps gathering around your food at a picnic? Some wasps, such as yellow jacket wasps, will feed on human food if they can find it.

This wasp is eating some jam.

WACKY WASPS and BRILLIANT BEES

Wasps and bees make a buzzing sound when they fly. That's the sound of their four wings flapping around 200 times in one second. That's so fast that we can't see each flap.

You might know a lot about bees, but did you know that they have some awesome dance moves? Honey bees perform a 'waggle dance' to let others know where to find food. They shake their bodies in the shape of an eight very quickly.

Time to EXPLORE

Well, that's the end of your training. Good news – you've passed! You are now ready to go out and explore the wilderness, armed with your new knowledge. Here is your well-earned explorer's badge. Well done, explorer!

Use a phone or tablet to scan the QR code below to download and print out your Bees & Wasps Expert badge. If you don't have one already, ask an adult to download a free QR code scanner from wherever you usually get your apps.

QUESTIONS

1:    Do wasps and bees have backbones?

2:    Where do bees find nectar and pollen?
- a) From humans
- b) From plants
- c) From the queen

3:    Where do bumble bees live?

4:    Can you think of three things a wasp likes to eat?

5:    What is your favourite thing about a bee or a wasp?

BookLife
freedom
Readers